TOP TEN FASTEST WONDERS ON EARTH

BY JOHN ALLAN

CONTENTS

WELCOME TO THE WORLD'S FASTEST!	4
FASTEST VEHICLE ON LAND	6
FASTEST CAR	8
FASTEST MOTORBIKE	10
FASTEST BIRD	12
FASTEST HUMAN	14
FASTEST-EATING ANIMAL	16
FASTEST AIRCRAFT	18
FASTEST TRAIN	20
FASTEST GROWING PLANT	22
FASTEST MAMMAL	24
FASTEST THING IN THE UNIVERSE	26
CLOSE, BUT NOT CLOSE ENOUGH!	28
THE PEOPLE BEHIND THE RECORDS	30
GLOSSARY	31
INDEX	32

Copyright © 2025 Hungry Tomato Ltd

First published in 2025 by Hungry Tomato Ltd
F15, Old Bakery Studios, Blewetts Wharf, Malpas Road, Truro, Cornwall, TR1 1QH, UK.

No part of this publication may be reproduced, stored in a retrieval system, or transmitted in any form or by any means, electronic, mechanical, photocopying, recording, or otherwise, without prior written permission of the copyright owner.

A CIP catalogue record for this book is available from the British Library.

ISBN 9781835694244

Printed in China

Discover more at
www.hungrytomato.com

Words in **BOLD** can be found in the glossary.

WELCOME TO THE WORLD'S FASTEST!

We live on a planet with so many impressive things. Prepare to be amazed by some of the world's speediest record-breakers...

MADE BY HUMANS AND NATURE

The fastest things in the world come in all shapes and sizes. Some are incredible animals with powerful bodies and unique features, and others are human-made speed machines.

MEASURING SPEED

You can usually see when something is super fast, but how can you tell exactly how fast it is? Speed is measured by working out how far a specific thing could travel in an hour. This is usually written as miles, or kilometres (km), per hour.

THE RECORD-BREAKERS

For human-made records, machines of the same type are all tested the same way to make sure they're given a fair chance. The test requirements are different for different machines. For example, cars complete two speed tests, and the **average** speed is the one that counts.

HOLDING ONTO A RECORD

People around the world are always competing to build even more powerful machines to try and break records and make history. This means that records and stats are constantly changing for human-made speed machines.

This book showcases 10 of the fastest things in the world!
It's hard to compare these record-breakers as they are all so different. What's fast for an animal may seem slow compared to a machine, but it's still impressive. The top 10 in this book are in no particular order, but everyone will have a favourite!

1 FASTEST VEHICLE ON LAND

For more than 100 years, people have tried to break records to travel the fastest on land.

The world land speed record is held by Thrust SSC – a **supersonic** car that is powered by two jet engines. In 1997, Thrust SSC not only broke the land speed record by reaching 763.035 miles per hour (1,227.985 km/h), it broke the **sound barrier** – it moved faster than the speed of sound!

This impressive car **accelerated** from 0 to 600 miles per hour (0-966 km/h) in 16 seconds! It has held its speed record for more than 25 years. A few people have come close, but none have beaten it yet.

DID YOU KNOW?

The record-breaking Thrust SSC was driven by a pilot called Andy Green. The famous drive took place on the flat Black Rock Desert in Nevada, USA.

ANDY GREEN

SUPER FACT

When something breaks the sound barrier, it creates a sonic boom – an incredibly loud sound like an explosion, which is caused by the shockwave that follows something moving that fast.

2 FASTEST CAR

New and faster cars are developed every year. The Bugatti Chiron Super Sport 300+ is currently the fastest production car in the world.

The Bugatti Chiron Super Sport 300+ can accelerate from 0 to 60 miles per hour (0-97 km/h) in 2.4 seconds, and reach a top speed of 304.7 miles per hour (490 km/h). This makes it so fast that it's considered a **hypercar**.

The Super Sport 300+ is more powerful than any supercar before it, thanks to its four big **turbochargers**. This means its engine produces almost 1,600 **horsepower**!

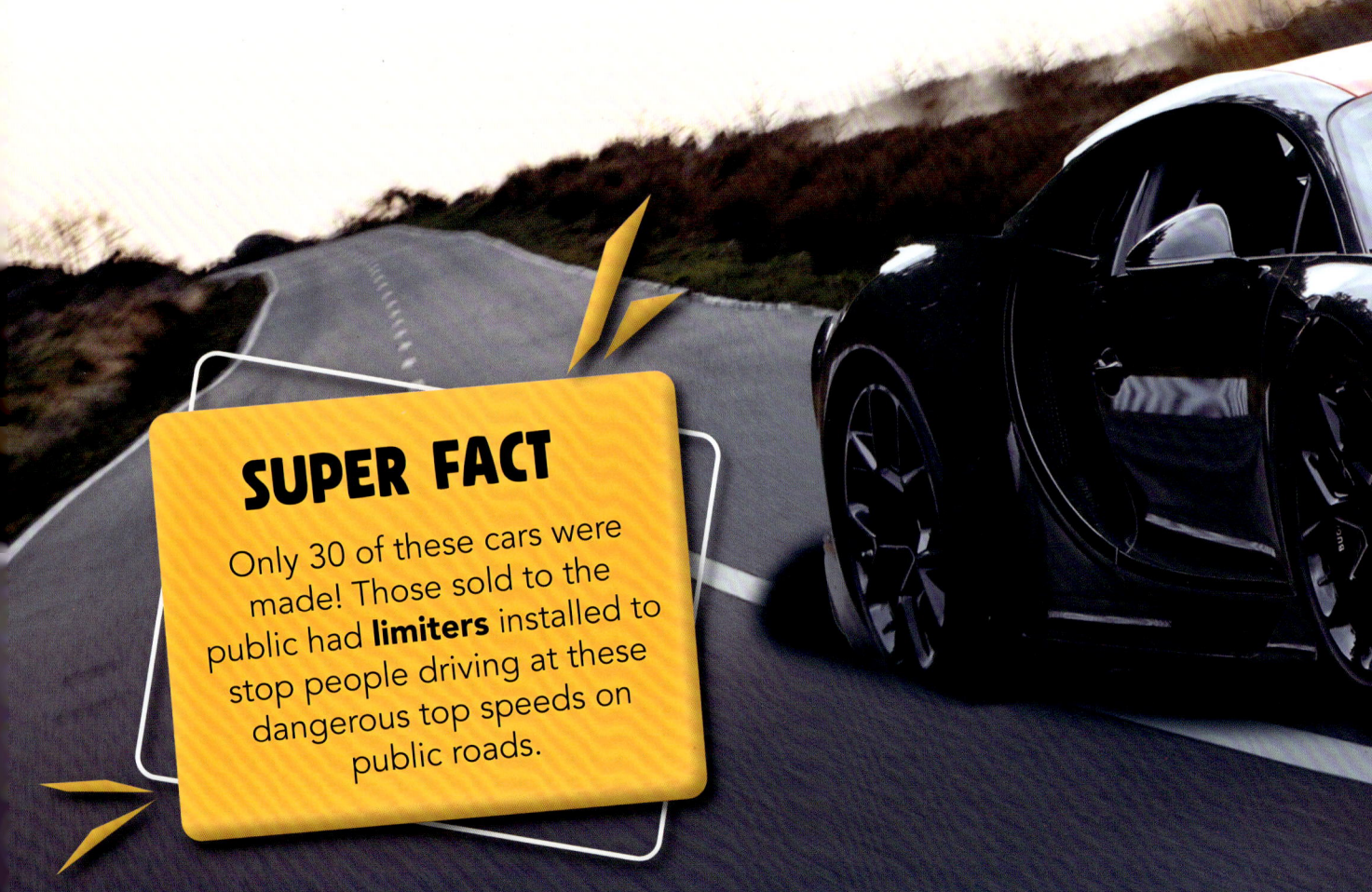

SUPER FACT

Only 30 of these cars were made! Those sold to the public had **limiters** installed to stop people driving at these dangerous top speeds on public roads.

DID YOU KNOW?

Some people argue this car shouldn't hold its speed record as it was only tested once, whereas other speed record attempts are tested twice. However, it's still the top speed ever reached by this type of car.

3 FASTEST MOTORBIKE

Many bikes have fought for the title, with records being broken all the time, but the current record for world's fastest production motorbike goes to the MTT 420-RR.

DID YOU KNOW?

The MTT Y2K, which preceded the 420-RR, was the first turbine-powered street legal production motorbike!

MTT Y2K TURBINE MOTORBIKE

This sleek bike has an incredible top speed of 275 miles per hour (443 km/h), thanks to its Rolls Royce **jet turbine** engine – an engine that is usually used in helicopters! The MTT 420-RR may be big, but it's very light because its body is made of aluminium and carbon fibre, materials which don't weigh very much. This is another reason it can go so fast!

It's a much more powerful version of the MTT Y2K which reached a top speed of 227 miles per hour (365 km/h).

SUPER FACT

The company that built the bike, Marine Turbine Technologies, claims this bike can go "Faster than you will ever dare to go!".

4 FASTEST BIRD

The peregrine falcon is the fastest bird on Earth. It can dive for prey at more than 200 miles per hour (322 km/h).

Its body is perfectly shaped to swoop through the air. Its curved wings help increase movement, **lift**, and speed during normal flight, and can be pulled tightly against its body to create a **streamlined** shape when diving. This allows the falcon to be more **aerodynamic** and increase its speed.

This falcon's strong heart beats up to 900 times per minute.
This helps with circulation and stops it from getting tired easily. All these things help the peregrine falcon move much faster than the fastest land animal (see pages 24-25).

DID YOU KNOW?

Male and female peregrine falcons look very similar, but the females are usually bigger than the males, and the male usually have whiter chests with hints of pink.

FEMALE

MALE

SUPER FACT

This falcon gives its name to one of the world's fastest motorbikes. The word "Hayabusa" is Japanese for "peregrine falcon".

5 FASTEST HUMAN

The record for the fastest human running speed goes to Usain Bolt, an eight-time Olympic champion known for his super sprinting speed.

Usain Bolt has beaten world records more than once! At the 2008 Olympics, he broke the records for the 100, 200, and 4 x 100-metre relays, running at 9.69 seconds, 19.3 seconds, and 37.1 seconds respectively. He was the first person ever to set world records in all three events!

At the 2009 World Championships, he ran even faster, breaking his own 100-metre record with a 9.58 second time! Usain Bolt retired from athletics in 2017, but he still holds the record for the 100 and 200 metres.

DID YOU KNOW?

Usain Bolt is also famous for his signature victory pose.

SUPER FACT

It was always thought that tall people are better at distance running than sprinting, as it takes them longer to build speed. Being 6 feet 5 inches tall (1.96 metres), Usain Bolt is taller than the average sprinter and defied this opinion.

6 FASTEST-EATING ANIMAL

The star-nosed mole has incredibly fast reaction times. It wins the award for fastest eater among mammals.

Scientists have recorded evidence that it usually only takes the star-nosed mole 230 **milliseconds** from identifying food as something that it can eat to capturing it and eating it. The fastest ever time recorded was only 120 milliseconds!

These North American creatures live in burrows underground, and in swampy areas. They mostly eat worms, snails, small fish, and insects. Because they're so quick, they can eat 5 pieces of **prey** in one second!

DID YOU KNOW?

This animal is a very well-adapted hunter: it is one of the few animals that can smell underwater; its front feet are strong and excellent for digging through soil; and its nose is the most sensitive organ of any animal — it's five times more sensitive than human "touch" senses.

SUPER FACT

The star-nosed mole gets its name from its 22-pronged nose. It helps the mole to sniff out and feel around for prey, which is helpful in its dark, underground home.

7 FASTEST AIRCRAFT

Aircraft are the fastest machines humans have invented by far! Although new aircraft are being built all the time, the record for the fastest aircraft is still held by the X-43A.

The X-43A is the fastest jet-powered aircraft ever built. It was an experimental, **unmanned** aircraft created by scientists at NASA that only flew once. It flew in 2004, when it hit 7,000 miles per hour (11,265 km/h)!

SUPER FACT

Speed is normally measured in miles or km per hour, but as aircraft fly so fast, scientists use a bigger unit of measurement – they compare things with the speed of sound. An aircraft flying at the speed of sound is said to fly at Mach 1. X-43A flew at Mach 9.6!

DID YOU KNOW?

X-43A took off mid-air, by being dropped by a bigger plane into the sky! A booster rocket shot the X-43 forwards, then its own engine took over and it reached its record-breaking speed.

8 FASTEST TRAIN

The fastest type of train in the world is the futuristic-looking, high-speed Maglev train. Its name stands for "magnetic levitation".

Super strong magnets are used to lift the train above a special track. Then magnets are used to guide and move the train. Because there is no **friction** from the train on the tracks, it's able to reach much higher speeds than "ordinary" trains.

The fastest speed recorded for a maglev train was 375 miles per hour (603 km/h) during a test run in Japan. Maglev trains that are used to transport people regularly have an average speed closer to 185 miles per hour (300 km/h).

Maglev trains use **electromagnets**. These are different from magnets you may use on your fridge!

Electromagnets are often used inside electronic machines, but the ones in maglev trains have been modified to be 10 times stronger!

DID YOU KNOW?

It's thought that maglev trains should operate better in harsh weather, like snow and ice, as they don't touch the tracks. However, this hasn't been properly tested yet.

9 FASTEST GROWING PLANT

The record for fastest growing plant in the world is held by bamboo, a woody, evergreen type of plant.

There are more than 1,000 different types of bamboo in the world. The fastest of them can grow up to almost 1 metre (3 ft) in a day! Scientists think they grow so fast because, unlike normal trees, bamboo stalks are hollow and they don't grow many leaves. This means the plant can put more of its energy towards growing its stalk.

The tallest type of bamboo can grow to be almost 30 metres (100 ft) tall. That's the same as a 10-storey building!

DID YOU KNOW?

Bamboo is important for wildlife. Although many animals rely on bamboo as a source of food, it's the only thing that pandas eat! Without it, they would go hungry.

SUPER FACT

Bamboo is very strong, so it's often used to make buildings and furniture. It can also be used to make smaller things like walking sticks, toothbrushes, chopsticks, and lots more!

10 FASTEST MAMMAL

The world's fastest mammal is the cheetah. These powerful predators can reach incredible speeds of 75 miles per hour (120 km/h) over short distances.

Cheetahs are not only fast, but they can accelerate at impressive speed. They have been recorded to accelerate from 0 to 60 miles per hour (0-97 km/h) in under 3 seconds. That's much faster than most cars!

Every part of a cheetah is designed for speed: it has a long, streamlined body which helps it cut through the air; special paws and claws which help it push off from the ground; and a flexible spine which works like a spring for its legs.

DID YOU KNOW?

Cheetahs' tails make up more than half of their overall length. This helps when chasing prey – their tails help them stay balanced and turn corners really quickly.

SUPER FACT

Cheetahs may be the fastest land animals, but they can only keep up these super speeds over short distances.

FASTEST THING IN THE UNIVERSE

You've now heard about 10 of the most incredibly fast things in the world. But what about the fastest thing in the universe?

The fastest thing in the universe is light, which travels at 299,792,458 metres (938,571,056 feet per second) per second in a **vacuum**!

SUPER FACT

The speed of light is about a million times faster than the speed of sound. That's why you see lightning before you hear it!

Astronomers use the speed of light to measure the distance between Earth and faraway stars and **galaxies**. One light-year is the distance that light travels in one year, and it's the same as 5,900,000,000,000 miles (9,495,129,600,000 km).

This means that when we look at stars shining in the sky, we are really looking back in time to when light left those places. They may not be there anymore!

DID YOU KNOW?

It takes an average of 8 minutes and 20 seconds for light from the Sun to reach Earth.

CLOSE, BUT NOT CLOSE ENOUGH!

There are lots of impressively fast things on Earth that didn't quite make our top ten. Here are some incredible runners-up.

FASTEST SPACECRAFT

Spacecraft can reach amazing speeds. The fastest to date is the Parker Solar Probe which, while orbiting close to the Sun, reached 364,660 miles per hour (586,860 km/h)!

FASTEST ROLLERCOASTER

The Formula Rossa in Ferrari World in Abu Dhabi, UAE, is the fastest rollercoaster in the world. It reaches its top speed of 149 miles per hour (240 km/h) in only 4.9 seconds!

FASTEST SPEED ACHIEVED BY HUMANS

The crew of Apollo 10, who went on a mission to the Moon in 1969, became the fastest humans in history when they flew at 24,790 miles per hour (39,895 km/h) on their flight back to Earth.

FASTEST STAR

The fastest star in the Milky Way (so far) is named S4714. It orbits the **supermassive black hole** at the middle of our galaxy at an estimated speed of 53.7 million miles per hour (86.4 million km/h).

MILKY WAY GALAXY

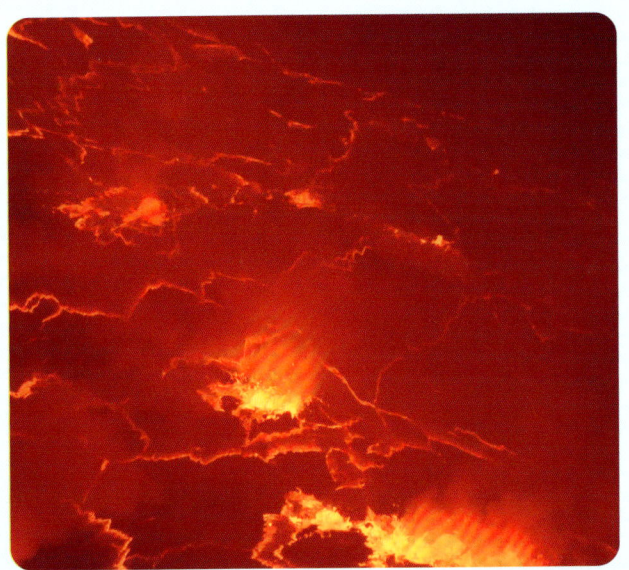

FASTEST LAVA FLOW

The lava from the eruption of Mount Nyiragongo in the Democratic Republic of the Congo in 1977 was the fastest-flowing lava ever recorded! It flowed out of the volcano with speeds up to 62 miles per hour (100 km/h).

THE PEOPLE BEHIND THE RECORDS

Humans have made some incredible, record-breaking machines throughout history. Here's just some of the people behind the amazing records in this book.

RICHARD NOBLE

Richard Noble designed Thrust SSC, the car that holds the world land speed record. He was also the driver of Thrust2, which broke the land speed record before Thrust SSC!

ANDY WALLACE

Andy Wallace is the driver who drove the Bugatti Chiron Super Sport 300+ through the 300 miles per hour (483 km/h) barrier to confirm it as the fastest car in the world. Andy is Bugatti's official test driver, and a celebrated racing driver.

OLE RØEMER

One of the first accurate measurements of the speed of light was done by Ole Røemer, a Danish astronomer, in the 1600s. He did it by recording the eclipses of Jupiter's moon, Io.

GLOSSARY

Accelerated – sped up.

Aerodynamic – something that is shaped to fly through the air more easily.

Average – the middle value of a set of numbers. If a car measures 100 miles per hour on one test run and 150 on the other, its average speed would be 125 miles per hour.

Electromagnets – a magnet that produces a magnetic field when electricity flows through it.

Friction – the force or resistance between two things when they are trying to slide across each other.

Galaxies – huge collections of gas, dust, stars, and planets. The Milky Way is the galaxy that Earth is in.

Horsepower – a unit of measurement which shows the power of a vehicle's engine.

Hypercar – a high-performance sportscar that has a more powerful engine and can achieve faster speeds than other sportscars or supercars.

Jet turbine – an engine that works by pulling air into a turbine and squeezing it before setting it alight with fuel. This creates a powerful backwards blast that turns another fan which controls the wheels.

Lift (in flight) – the force that holds something in the air.

Limiters – safety devices that are fitted to vehicles to limit how fast they can go.

Mammals – warm-blooded animals (including humans) that produce milk to feed their young.

Milliseconds – one thousandths of a second.

Prey – an animal that is hunted by other animals.

Production car – a car that is produced in large quantities and made available for people to buy and drive on public roads.

Sound barrier – the speed at which sound travels. When something travels faster than sound, it is said to have broken the sound barrier.

Streamlined – something that is shaped to move through matter, like air or water, more easily.

Supermassive black hole – a black hole that is more than 100,000 times the mass of the Sun.

Supersonic – something that moves faster than the speed of sound.

Turbochargers – devices that boost an engine's power.

Unmanned – something that does not have people inside it. This is usually used to refer to vehicles.

Vacuum – a space that has absolutely nothing in it – not even air.

INDEX

A
Animals
    Cheetah 24-25
    Panda 22
    Peregrine falcon 12-13
    Star-nosed mole 16-17
Apollo 10 mission 29

B
Bamboo 22-23
Black Rock Desert, Nevada, USA 6
Bolt, Usain 14-15
Bugatti Chiron Super Sport 300+ car 8-9, 30

F
Ferrari World, Abu Dhabi, UAE 28
Formula Rossa rollercoaster 28

G
Green, Andy 6

H
Hayabusa motorbike 13

L
Land speed record 6, 30

M
Maglev train 20-21
Marine Turbine Industries 11
Mount Nyiragongo, Democratic Republic of the Congo 29
MTT Y2K 10-11
MTT 420-RR 10-11

N
NASA 18
Noble, Richard 30

O
Olympics 14
Outer space 26-27, 28-29

P
Parker Space Probe 28

R
Rocket 19
Røemer, Ole 30

S
Speed of light 26-27, 30
Speed of sound 6-7, 18, 26, 31
S4714 star 29

T
Thrust SSC 6-7, 30

W
Wallace, Andy 30
World Championships 14

X
X-43A aircraft 14-15

Picture credits:
Abbreviations: m-middle, t-top, l-left, r-right, bg-background.

Wikipedia: By NASA - http://antwrp.gsfc.nasa.gov/apod/ap040329.html [1]Catalogue: http://www.dfrc.nasa.gov/Gallery/Photo/X-43A/HTML/ED99-45243-01.htmlTransferred from en.wikipedia to Commons by TheDJ using CommonsHelper 1bg, 5br, 18-19bg, 32b; By Supermac1961 from CHAFFORD HUNDRED, England, https://commons.wikimedia.org/w/index.php?curid=18197508 8ml; By NASA/Johns Hopkins APL/Steve Gribben - http://parkersolarprobe.jhuapl.edu/Multimedia/Images.php, 28ml; By NASA - https://images.nasa.gov/details/S69-32613http://grin.hq.nasa.gov/IMAGES/LARGE/GPN-2000-001163.jpg on the Wayback Machine at the Wayback Machinehttp://grin.hq.nasa.gov/ABSTRACTS/GPN-2000-001163.html on the Wayback Machine at the Wayback Machine 29tl; By ian mcwilliams - originally posted to Flickr as Richard Noble - former World Land Speed Record holder, CC BY 2.0 30tl; By Jaguar MENA - Jaguar XJ l Night and Day with Andy Wallace, CC BY 2.0 30mr; By Jacob Coning - Farvereproduktioner efter 20 portrætter af berømte danske mænd (København 1943) 30bl. NASA: images-assets.nasa.gov/image/EC01-0084-5/EC01-0084-5~orig.jpg 19br; images-assets.nasa.gov/image/PIA10748/PIA10748~orig.jpg 29mr. Shutterstock: 4ml, 12-13bg, 12b, 25bg; 1933 media productions 5tl (car), 8-9bg (car); Agnieszka Bacal 16br, 17bg; Andrew Harken (Andy Green) 6br; Cyo Bo 20-21b; Anna Kucherova 22b; Danita Delimont 6b (navada); Elena Erasmus 24br; Focus Pix 14b; Kaliva 15bg; Kiki Dohmeier 29bl; Leungchopan 23bg; Lukasz Pawel Szczepansky 25mr; Patruflo 7bg; Pit Stock 28br; Pixel-Shot 9tr; Sanket27 5tl (background), 8-9bg (Background); Sergii_Petruk 21mr; slowmotiongli 2-3bg; Triff 4br, 26-27bg.

Every effort has been made to trace the copyright holders, and we apologise in advance for any unintentional omissions. We would be pleased to insert the appropriate acknowledgements in any subsequent edition of this publication.